Need For Speed
JETS

MICHAEL SHARPE

Published in 2009 by TAJ Books International LLP

27, Ferndown Gardens,
Cobham,
Surrey,
UK,
KT11 2BH

www.tajbooks.com

ISBN-13: 978-1-84406-137-2

Printed in China.

Need For Speed
JETS

MICHAEL SHARPE

INTRODUCTION

The Heinkel He 178, the world's first aircraft to fly purely on turbojet power

A jet aircraft is an aircraft propelled by jet engines. Jet aircraft generally fly much faster than propeller-powered aircraft and at higher altitudes — as high as 10,000 to 15,000 meters (about 33,000 to 49,000 ft). At these altitudes, jet engines achieve maximum efficiency over long distances. The engines in propeller powered aircraft achieve their maximum efficiency at much lower altitudes. Jet aircraft can move faster than sound.

Henri Coand , a Romanian Engineer, was the first to build a jet plane in 1910 — the Coanda-1910. Later on, two engineers, Frank Whittle in the United Kingdom and Hans von Ohain in Germany, developed the concept independently during the late 1930s, although credit for the first turbojet is given to Whittle. The concept had already been discussed as early as August 1928 by Frank Whittle at Flying

School, Wittering, but Hans von Ohain also wrote in February 1936 to Ernst Heinkel, telling him of the design and its possibilities. However, it can be argued that A. A. Griffith, who published a paper in July 1926 on compressors and turbines, which he had been studying at the RAE, also deserves priority credit, perhaps more than either Frank Whittle or Hans von Ohain.

The first turbine-equipped jetplane was designed on paper in late 1929 when Frank Whittle of the British Royal Air Force sent his concept to the Air Ministry to see if it would be of any interest to them. The first manufactured turbine jetplane was the Heinkel He 178 turbojet prototype of the German Air Force (Luftwaffe), piloted by Erich Warsitz on August 27, 1939.

The first flight of the Italian Caproni Campini N.1 motorjet prototype

A Memorial to Sir Frank Whittle on the northern boundary of Farnborough Aerodrome UK and showing a full-scale model of the Gloster E28/39

was on August 27, 1940. Test pilot Major Mario De Bernardi of the Regia Aeronautica was at the controls.

The British flew their Gloster E.28/39 prototype on May 15, 1941, powered by Sir Frank Whittle's turbojet, and piloted by Flt Lt PG Sayer. When the United States learned of the British work, it produced the Bell XP-59 with a version of the Whittle engine built by General Electric, which flew on September 12, 1942, piloted by Col L. Craigie.

The first operational jet fighter was the Messerschmitt Me 262, made by Germany during late World War II. It was the fastest conventional aircraft of World War II — although the rocket-powered Messerschmitt Me 163 Komet was faster. Mass production started in 1944, too late for a decisive effect on the outcome of the war. About the same time, the United Kingdom's Gloster Meteor was limited to defense of the UK

against the V1 flying bomb and ground-attack operations over Europe in the last months of the war. The Imperial Japanese Navy also developed jet aircraft in 1945, including the Nakajima J9Y Kikka, a crude copy of the Me-262

On November 8, 1950, during the Korean War, United States Air Force Lt. Russell J. Brown, flying in an F-80, intercepted two North Korean MiG-15s near the Yalu River and shot them down in the first jet-to-jet dogfight in history.

BOAC operated the first commercial jet service, from London to Johannesburg, in 1952 with the de Havilland Comet jetliner.

The fastest military jet plane was the SR-71 Blackbird at Mach 3.2. The fastest commercial jet plane was the Tupolev Tu-144 at Mach 2.35.

The fastest military jet plane was the SR-71 Blackbird at Mach 3.2.

Modern airliners cruise at speeds of 0.75 to 0.85 Mach, or 75% to 85% of the speed of sound (420 to 580 mph/ 680-900 km/h). The speed of sound predominantly depends on air temperature (hardly at all on pressure), so the Mach number for the speed of a jet also varies with atmospheric conditions. NASA and the US Federal Aviation Administration have been promoting Very Light Jets: small general aviation aircraft seating 4 to 8 passengers. A jet airliner is a passenger airplane that is powered by jet engines. This term is sometimes contracted to jetliner. In contrast to today's relatively fuel-efficient, turbofan-powered air travel, first generation jet airliner travel was noisy and fuel inefficient. These inefficiencies were addressed by the invention of turboprop and turbofan engines. The first airliners with turbojet propulsion were experimental conversions of the Avro

Lancastrian piston engined airliner, which were flown with several types of early jet engine, including the de Havilland Ghost and the Rolls-Royce Nene, however these retained the two inboard piston engines, the jets being housed in the outboard nacelles and these aircraft were therefore of 'mixed' propulsion. The first airliner with full jet power was the Nene-powered Vickers VC.1 Viking G-AJPH, which first flew on the 6 April 1948. The first purpose-built jet airliner was the de Havilland Comet which first flew in 1949 and entered service in 1952. Also developed in 1949 was the Avro Jetliner, and although it never reached production, the term jetliner caught on as a generic term for all passenger jet aircraft.

These first jet airliners were followed some years later by the Sud Aviation Caravelle, Tupolev Tu-104 (2nd in service), Boeing 707,

The fastest commercial jet plane was the Tupolev Tu-144 at Mach 2.35.

Douglas DC-8, and Convair 880. National prestige was attached to developing prototypes and bringing these first generation designs into service. There was also a strong nationalism in purchasing policy, such that the Boeing and Douglas products became closely associated with Pan Am, while BOAC ordered British made Comets.

These two airlines with strong nautical traditions of command hierarchy rank and chain of command, retained from their days of operations with flying boats, undoubtably were quick to capitalize upon, with the help of advertising agencies, the linkings of the "speed of jets" with the safety and secure "luxury of ocean liners" among public perception.

Aeroflot used Russian Tupolevs, while Air France introduced French Caravelles. Commercial realities dictated exceptions, however, as few airlines could risk missing out on a superior product: American airlines ordered the pioneering Comet (but later cancelled when the Comet ran into fatigue problems), Canadian, British and European airlines could not ignore the better operating economics of the Boeing 707 and the DC-8, while some American airlines ordered the Caravelle.

Boeing became the most successful of the early manufacturers. The KC-135 Stratotanker and military versions of the 707 remain operational, mostly as tankers or freighters. The basic configuration of the Boeing, Convair and Douglas aircraft jet airliner designs, with widely spaced podded engines under slung on pylons beneath a swept wing, proved to be the most common arrangement and was most easily compatible with the large-diameter high-bypass turbofan engines that subsequently prevailed for reasons of quietness and fuel efficiency.

INTRODUCTION

The Lockheed JetStar one of the first business jets, shown here is Elvis Presleys at Graceland.

The de Havilland and Tupolev designs had engines incorporated within the wings next to the fuselage, a concept that endured only within military designs while the Caravelle pioneered engines mounted either side of the rear fuselage.In the 1960s, when jet airliners were powered by slim, low-bypass engines, many aircraft used the rear-engined, T-tail configuration, such as the BAC One-Eleven, Douglas DC-9 twinjets ; Boeing 727, Hawker Siddeley Trident, Tupolev Tu-154 trijets; and the paired multi-engined Ilyushin Il-62, and Vickers VC-10 whose engines were mounted upon the aft fuselage. This engine arrangement survives into the 21st century on numerous twin engined Douglas DC-9 derivatives plus newer short haul and range turbofan powered regional aircraft such as the "regional jet airliners" built by Bombardier, Embraer and, until recently, Fokker. However other

"jetliner" developments, such as the concept of rocket assisted takeoffs RATO, and the briefly mentioned water-injection as used and tested upon first generation passenger jets, as well as trailing edge mounted powerplants, afterburners also known as reheat used upon supersonic jetliners SSTs such as the Concorde and Tupolev Tu-144, likewise have been relegated to the past. For business jets, the rear-engined universal configuration pioneered by the turbojet powered early Learjet 23, North American Sabreliner, and Lockheed JetStar is common practice on smaller bizjet aircraft as the wing is too close to the ground to accommodate underslung engines. This is as opposed to early generation jet airliners, whose design engineers slung jet engines on the rear to increase wing lift performance and at the same time reduce cabin noise of the lower bypass "turbojet" engines.

The Cessna Mustang an example of the VLJ (Very Light Jet)

Airliner descriptions are commonly broken down into the distinctions of the generally long-haul civilian passenger jumbo and, widebody jet airliners, and short-haul civilian passenger "jet" airliners. Among some of these categories included among the short-haul civilian passenger "jets" are both longer and shorter ranged "narrow-body jet and regional jet types." Semantically, the terms "civilian" "turbine powered" "jet" "passenger" "air" "liner" aircraft are routinely dropped from these various terms to accurately describe "jet aircraft" which can lead to confusion among those practicing language purity.

Almost all production business jets, such as General Dynamics' Gulfstream and the Gates Lear Jet (now built by Bombardier), have had two or three engines, though the Jetstar, an early business jet, had four. Advances in engine reliability and power have rendered four-engine designs obsolete, and only Dassault Aviation still builds three-engine models (in the Falcon line). The emerging market for so-called "very light jets" and "personal jets", has seen the introduction (at least on paper) of several single-engine designs as well.

Almost all business jets have rear-mounted engines, because the wing (mounted low for performance reasons) is too near the ground for engines to be slung underneath it.

Airliners are sometimes converted into luxury business jets. Such converted aircraft are often used by celebrities with a large entourage or press corps, or by sports teams, but airliners often face operational restrictions based on runway length or local noise restrictions.

A focus of development is at the low end of the market with small models, many far cheaper than existing business jets. Many of these

INTRODUCTION

fall into the very light jet (VLJ) category and are used by the air taxi industry. Cessna has developed the Mustang, a six-place twinjet (2 crew + 4 passengers) available for $2.55 million USD. A number of smaller manufacturers have planned even cheaper jets; the first is the Eclipse 500 which has become available at around 1.5 million USD. It remains to be seen whether the new jet manufacturers will complete their designs, or find the market required to sell their jets at the low prices planned.

There are approximately 11,000 business jets in the worldwide fleet with the vast majority of them based in the United States or owned by US companies. The European market is the next largest, with growing activity in the Middle East, Asia, and Central America. Because new aircraft orders can take two to three years for delivery, there is a large pre-owned marketplace with immediate availability. Since 1996 the term "fractional jet" has been used in connection with business aircraft owned by a consortium of companies. Costly overheads such as flight crew, hangarage and maintenance can be shared through such arrangements. In addition to outright new or pre-owned acquisition by aircraft users, new business jets are often purchased using a system of ownership positions. Usually this entails a deposit that reserves a

future delivery of the aircraft: a "position" of ownership for a future date, normally three to five years in in advance. Additional deposits are paid as the aircraft nears completion. The future positions can be bought and sold by the owners, with any remaining balances due to the manufacturer. There is an active market in aircraft positions, and during turbulent economic times, these positions are sometimes abandoned, leaving the manufacturer with the deposit funds, but also the need to sell the aircraft position to another buyer. Most people use the term 'jet aircraft' to denote gas turbine based airbreathing jet engines, but rockets and scramjets are both also propelled by them. The fastest airbreathing jet aircraft is the unmanned X-43 scramjet at around Mach 9-10, shown below. The fastest manned (rocket) aircraft is the X-15 at Mach 6.85. The Space Shuttle, while far faster than the X-43 or X-15, is not regarded as a jet aircraft during ascent, nor during reentry and landing (as it is unpowered during this phase of operation).

The aircraft featured on the following pages are in order of flying speed, the fastest to the slowest.

X-43A

The X-43 is an unmanned experimental hypersonic aircraft design with multiple planned scale variations meant to test different aspects of hypersonic flight. It is part of NASA's Hyper-X program. A winged booster rocket with the X-43 itself at the tip, called a "stack", is launched from a carrier plane. After the booster rocket (a modified first stage of the Pegasus rocket) brings the stack to the target speed and altitude, it is discarded, and the X-43 flies free using its own engine, a scramjet. The third flight of the X-43A set a new speed record of 12,144 km/h (7,536 mph), or Mach 9.6, on November 16, 2004. It was boosted by a modified Pegasus rocket which was launched from a Boeing B-52 at 13,157 meters (43,166 ft). After a free flight where the scramjet operated for about ten seconds, the craft made a planned crash into the Pacific Ocean off the coast of southern California. The most recent success in the X-plane series of aircraft, the X-43 is part of NASA's Hyper-X program, involving the American space agency and contractors such as Boeing, MicroCraft Inc, Orbital Sciences Corporation and General Applied Science Laboratory (GASL). MicroCraft Inc., now known as ATK GASL, built the X-43A and its engine. The Hyper-X Phase I is a NASA Aeronautics and Space Technology Enterprise program being conducted jointly by the Langley Research Center, Hampton, Virginia, and the Dryden Flight Research Center, Edwards, California. Langley is the lead center and is responsible for hypersonic technology development. Dryden is responsible for flight research.

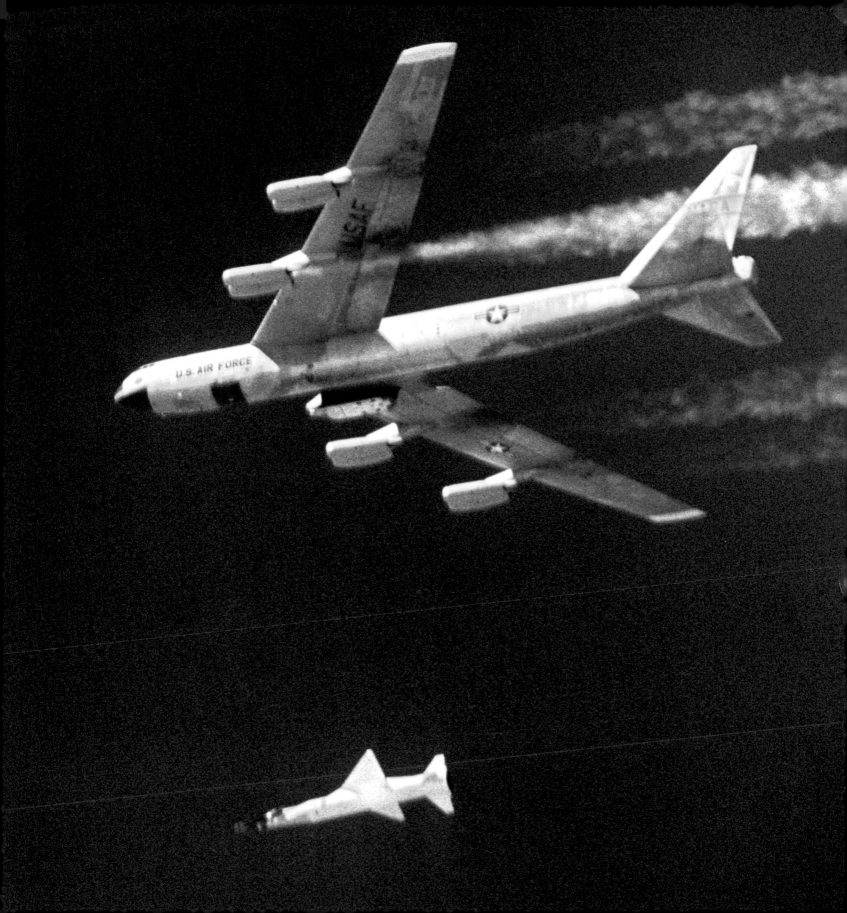

X-15

The North American X-15 rocket-powered aircraft was part of the X-series of experimental aircraft, initiated with the Bell X-1, that were made for the USAF, NASA, and the USN. The X-15 set speed and altitude records in the early 1960s, reaching the edge of outer space and returning with valuable data used in aircraft and spacecraft design. It currently holds the world record for the fastest speed ever reached by a manned aircraft. During the X-15 program, 13 of the flights (by eight pilots) met the USAF spaceflight criteria by exceeding the altitude of 50 miles (80.47 km. 264,000ft.), thus qualifying the pilots for astronaut status; some pilots also qualified for NASA astronaut wings. Of all the X-15 missions, two flights (by the same pilot) qualified as space flights, per the international FAI definition of a spaceflight by exceeding a 100 kilometer (62.137 mi, 328,084 ft) altitude.

The X-15 was based on a concept study from Walter Dornberger for the NACA for a hypersonic research aircraft. The requests for proposal were published on 30 December 1954 for the airframe and on 4 February 1955 for the rocket engine. The X-15 was built by two manufacturers: North American Aviation was contracted for the airframe in November 1955, and Reaction Motors was contracted for building the engines in 1956. The first X-15 flight was an unpowered test flight by Scott Crossfield, on 8 June 1959; he also piloted the first powered flight, on 17 September 1959, with his first XLR-99 flight on 15 November 1960. The two XLR-11 rocket engines for the initial X-15A model delivered 72kN (16,000 lbf) of total thrust; the main engine (installed later) was a single XLR-99 rocket engine delivering 254kN (57,000 lbf) at sea level, and 311 kN (70,000 lbf) at peak altitude.

SPACESHIP ONE

SpaceShipOne is a spaceplane that completed the first privately funded human spaceflight on June 21, 2004. It was developed by Scaled Composites. SpaceShipOne was an experimental air-launched suborbital spaceplane that used a hybrid rocket motor. The design featured a unique "feathering" reentry system where the rear half of the wing and the twin tail booms folded upward along a hinge running the length of the wing; this increased drag while remaining stable. The achievements of SpaceShipOne are more comparable to the X-15 than orbiting spacecraft like the Space Shuttle. Accelerating a spacecraft to orbital speed requires more than 60 times as much energy as lifting it to 100 km.

SpaceShipOne was developed by Scaled Composites, Burt Rutan's aviation company, in their Tier One program, without government funding. On June 21, 2004, it made the first privately funded human spaceflight, and on October 4, it won the $10-million Ansari X PRIZE, by reaching 100 kilometers in altitude twice in a two-week period with the equivalent of three people on board, with no more than ten percent of the non-fuel weight of the spacecraft replaced between flights. Development costs were estimated to be $25-million, funded completely by Paul Allen. During its testing regimen, SpaceShipOne set a number of important "firsts", including first privately funded aircraft to exceed Mach 2 and Mach 3, first privately funded manned spacecraft to exceed 100km altitude, and first privately funded reusable spacecraft. SpaceShipOne is registered with the FAA as N328KF. 'N' is the prefix for US-registered aircraft; '328KF' was chosen by Scaled Composites to stand for 328 kilo feet (about 100 kilometers), the officially designated edge of space.

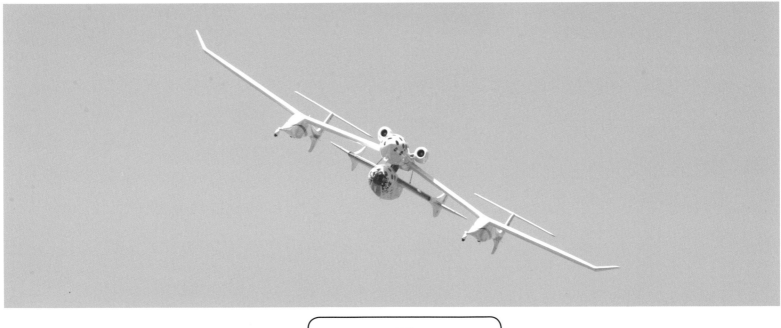

LOCKHEED SR-71

The Lockheed SR-71, unofficially known as the Blackbird and by its crews as the Habu, was an advanced, long-range, Mach 3 strategic reconnaissance aircraft developed from the Lockheed YF-12A and A-12 aircraft by the Lockheed Skunk Works (also responsible for the U-2 and many other advanced aircraft). It flew from 1964 - 1998. The legendary "Kelly" Johnson, in particular, was the man behind many of the design's advanced concepts. The SR-71 was one of the first aircraft to be shaped to have an extremely low radar signature. The aircraft flew so fast and so high that if the pilot detected a surface-to-air missile launch, the standard evasive action was simply to accelerate. No SR-71 was ever shot down. The SR-71's Pratt & Whitney J58 engines never exceeded testbench values above Mach 3.6 in unclassified tests. Given the history of the plane, the advanced and classified nature of much of its original design, and most importantly, the simple fact that no SR-71 exists in a form that is immediately airworthy, it may never be known what the true design tolerances of the aircraft were, or if these tolerances were ever approached in flight. This unverifiability undoubtedly contributes to the myths and fallacies surrounding the SR-71. The SR-71 was the first operational aircraft designed around a stealthy shape and materials. The most visible marks of its low radar cross section (RCS) are its inwardly-canted vertical stabilizers and the fuselage chines. Comparably, a plane of the SR-71's size should generate a radar image the size of a flying barn, but its actual return is more like that of a single door. Though with a much smaller RCS than expected for a plane of its size, it was still easily detected, because the exhaust stream would return its own radar signature.

F-111

The General Dynamics F-111 is a long-range strategic bomber, reconnaissance, and tactical strike aircraft. The USAF variants were officially named Aardvark, their longtime USAF nickname, at their 1996 ceremony of retirement from that service. In Australian service the F-111 is known as the Pig. The F-111 project was long considered by some to be an expensive failure, but it eventually produced an outstanding deep interdiction/strike aircraft. The F-111's beginnings were in the TFX, an ambitious early 1960s project to combine the U.S. Air Force requirement for a fighter-bomber with the U.S. Navy's need for a long-range carrier defense fighter to replace the F-4 Phantom II and the F-8 Crusader. The fighter design philosophy of the day concentrated on very high speed, raw power, and air-to-air missiles.

In June 1960 the USAF issued a specification for a long-range interdiction/strike aircraft able to penetrate Soviet air defenses at very low altitudes and very high speeds to deliver tactical nuclear weapons against crucial Soviet targets like airfields and supply depots. Dogfighting maneuverability and cannon armament were considered of little importance. This would change within a few years as experience showed that close-in dogfighting remained important in air combat: guns and an emphasis on agility were reintroduced to fighter design, but only after the F-111 was developed. First flight of the F-111A, as the USAF version was designated, was 21 December 1964, and entry into service with the USAF began 18 July 1967. Currently the Royal Australian Air Force is the only operator of the F-111 and continues to upgrade the aircraft with modern avionics and weapon systems.

F-15 EAGLE

The Boeing (formerly McDonnell Douglas) F-15 Eagle is an American-built all-weather tactical fighter designed to gain and maintain air superiority in aerial combat. It first flew in July of 1972. A derivative of the aircraft is the F-15E Strike Eagle, a highly successful all-weather strike fighter which entered service in 1988. The F-15's maneuverability is derived from low wing loading (weight to wing area ratio) with a high thrust-to-weight ratio enabling the aircraft to turn tightly without losing airspeed. The F-15 can climb to 30,000 ft. in around 60 seconds. The weapons and flight control systems are designed so one person can safely and effectively perform air-to-air combat.

The F-15E Strike Eagle is a two-seat, dual-role, totally integrated fighter for all-weather, air-to-air and deep interdiction missions. The rear cockpit is upgraded to include four multi-purpose CRT displays for aircraft systems and weapons management. The digital, triple-redundant Lear Siegler flight control system permits coupled automatic terrain following, enhanced by a ring-laser gyro inertial navigation system. For low-altitude, high-speed penetration and precision attack on tactical targets at night or in adverse weather, the F-15E carries a high-resolution APG-70 radar and low-altitude navigation and targeting infrared for night pods.

F-22 RAPTOR

The F-22 Raptor is a stealth fighter aircraft built by Lockheed Martin Aeronautics and Boeing Integrated Defense Systems. It was originally envisioned as an air superiority fighter, but is equipped for ground attack, electronic attack, and signals intelligence roles as well. The Raptor's combat computer systems and power are unmatched by any other fighter planned to be developed by 2020. The AN/APG-77 AESA radar, designed for air-superiority and strike operations, features a low-observable, active-aperture, electronically-scanned array that can track multiple targets in all kinds of weather. The AN/APG-77 changes frequencies more than 1,000 times per second to reduce the chance of being intercepted. The radar can also focus its emissions to overload enemy sensors, giving the plane an electronic-attack capability. The radar's information is processed by the two Raytheon-built Common Integrated Processor (CIP)s. Each CIP operates at 10.5 billion instructions per second and has 300 megabytes of memory. Unprecedented amounts of information can be gathered from the radar and other onboard and offboard systems, filtered by the CIP, and offered in easy-to-digest ways on several cockpit displays, enabling the pilot to remain on top of complicated situations. The Raptor's software is composed of over 1.7 million lines of code, most of which concerns processing data from the radar. The Raptor is designed to carry air-to-air missiles in internal bays to avoid disrupting its stealth capability. Missiles are launched by hydraulic arms that hurl them away from the jet so quickly that the weapons-bay doors pop open for less than one second.

TUPOLEV TU-144

The Tupolev Tu-144 (NATO name: "Charger") was the world's first supersonic transport aircraft (SST, with its first flight preceding that of Concorde), constructed under the direction of the Soviet Tupolev design bureau headed by Alexei Tupolev. A prototype first flew on 31 December 1968 near Moscow, two months before the similar Aérospatiale / British Aircraft Corporation Concorde. The Tu-144 first broke the speed of sound on 5 June 1969, and on 15 July 1969 it became the first commercial transport to exceed Mach two, and it was at the time the fastest commercial-type airliner. The Tu-144 was Tupolev's only supersonic commercial airliner venture. Tupolev's other large supersonic aircraft were designed and built to military specifications. All these aircraft benefited from technical and scientific input from TsAGI, the Central Aerohydrodynamic Institute.

At the Paris Air Show on 3 June 1973, the development program of the Tu-144 suffered severely when the first Tu-144S production airliner (reg 77102) crashed. While in the air, the Tu-144 underwent a violent downwards maneuver. Trying to pull out of the subsequent dive, the Tu-144 broke up and crashed, destroying 15 houses and killing all six people on board the Tu-144 and eight more on the ground. The causes of this incident remain controversial to this day. A popular theory was that the Tu-144 was forced to avoid a French Mirage chase plane which was attempting to photograph its canards, which were very advanced for the time, and that the French and Soviet governments colluded with each other to cover up such details.

SU-27 FLANKER

The Sukhoi Su-27 (NATO reporting name 'Flanker') is originally a Soviet fighter aircraft designed by the Sukhoi Design Bureau (SDB). It was intended as a direct competitor for the new generation of American fighters (which emerged as the F-14 Tomcat, F-15 Eagle, F-16 Fighting Falcon, and F/A-18 Hornet), with exceptional range, heavy armament, and very high agility. The Su-27 most often flies air superiority missions, but is able to perform almost all combat operations. Some believe the Su-27 to have been born from a competition between Sukhoi and Mikoyan-Gurevich, given the Su-27's and Mikoyan MiG-29's similar shape. This is not so. The Su-27 was designed as long-range air superiority fighter and interceptor, whereas the MiG-29 was designed to fill the role of short-range tactical support fighter.

The Su-27's basic design is aerodynamically similar to the MiG-29, but it is substantially larger. It is a very large aircraft, and to mimimize its weight its structure has a high percentage of titanium (about 30%, more than any of its contemporaries). No composite materials were used. The swept wing blends into the fuselage at the leading edge extensions and is essentially a delta, although the tips are cropped for wingtip missile rails or ECM pods. The Su-27 is not a true delta, however, because it retains conventional tailplanes, with two vertical tailfins outboard of the engines, supplemented by two fold-down ventral fins for additional lateral stability. The Su-27's Lyulka AL-31F turbofan engines are widely spaced, both for safety reasons and to ensure uninterrupted airflow through the intakes. The space between the engines also provides additional lift, reducing wing loading.

F-14 TOMCAT

The Grumman F-14 Tomcat is a supersonic, twin-engine, two-seat, variable-sweep wing aircraft. The F-14 was the United States Navy's primary maritime air superiority fighter, fleet defense interceptor and tactical reconnaissance platform from 1974 to 2006. It later performed precision strike missions once it was integrated with the Low Altitude Navigation and Targeting Infrared for Night LANTIRN system. The F-14 was developed after the collapse of the F-111B project, and was the first of the American teen-series fighters which were designed incorporating the experience of air combat against MiGs during the Vietnam War.

The engines are fed by two rectangular air intakes located under the wings. These Pratt & Whitney JT10As (better known as the TF30) were relatively powerful for the time (5.670/9.480 kg/t) and being turbofans, they allowed reduced fuel consumption while cruising, which was important for long patrol missions. Both air intakes have movable ramps and bleed doors that are operated by the air data computer to enable enough air to enter the engine while keeping shockwaves away from the engine. The exhausts also feature variable nozzles with moving petals that open or close depending on engine state. The overall thrust-to-weight ratio at maximum load is around 0.56, which does not compare favorably with the F-15A's ratio of 0.85. Even so, the aircraft itself is able to reach Mach 2.4, and the maximum speed is officially Mach 2.34. Internal fuel capacity is 2,400 US gallons (9100 L): 290 US gallons (1,100 L) in each wing, 690 US gallons (2,600 L) in a series of tanks aft of the cockpit, and a further 457 US gallons (1,730 L) in two feeder tanks.

DASSAULT RAFALE

The Rafale is a French twin-engined delta-wing highly agile multi-role fighter aircraft designed and built by Dassault Aviation. Introduced in 2000, the Rafale is produced both for land-based use with the French Air Force and for carrier-based naval operations with the French Navy. In the mid-1970s, both the French Air Force and Navy had a requirement to find a new generation of fighter, and their requirements were similar enough to be merged into one project. Dassault considered cooperating in the development of the aircraft that was eventually called the Eurofighter Typhoon but the French government cited the need to field an aircraft sooner than Eurofighter.

The Rafale features a delta wing combined with active integrated (Close-coupled) canard to maximize maneuverability (withstanding +9g or -3g) while maintaining stability in flight, a maximum of 11g can be reached in case of emergency. The canard also reduces landing speed to 115 knots. According to internal sources, the low speed limit is 100kt but 80kt is sometimes demonstrated during airshows by pilots willing to underline low speed qualities of the aircraft. A minimum of 15 kt have been reached during simulated combat vs a Mirage 2000 by an aggressive pilot. The aircraft can operate from 400 meter runways.

SAAB GRIPEN

The Saab JAS 39 Gripen (Translated in English as Griffin) is a fighter aircraft manufactured by the Swedish aerospace company Saab. Gripen International acts as a prime contracting organisation and is responsible for marketing, selling and supporting the Gripen fighter around the world. The aircraft is in service with the Swedish Air Force, the Czech Air Force, the Hungarian Air Force and the South African Air Force, and has been ordered by the Royal Thai Air Force. A total of 236 Gripens have been ordered as of 2008.

One interesting feature is the Gripen's ability to take off and land on public roads, which was part of Sweden's war defence strategy. The aircraft is designed to be able to operate even if the air force does not have air superiority. During the Cold War, the Swedish Armed Forces were preparing to defend against a possible invasion from the Soviet Union. Even though the defensive strategy in principle called for an absolute defence of Swedish territory, military planners calculated that Swedish defence forces could eventually be overrun. For that reason, Sweden had military stores dispersed all over the country, in order to maintain the capacity of inflicting damage on the enemy even if military installations were lost. Accordingly, among the requirements from the Swedish Air Force was that the Gripen fighter should be able to land on public roads near military stores for quick maintenance, and take off again. As a result, the Gripen fighter can be refueled and re-armed in ten minutes by a five man mobile ground crew operating out of a truck, and then resume flying sorties.

MIG29 FULCRUM

The MiG-29, like the larger Sukhoi Su-27 'Flanker', began development in 1969, when the Soviet Union learned of the U.S. Air Force 'FX' program, which would eventually produce the F-15 Eagle. Even before the aircraft was developed, Soviet leadership realized that the new American fighter would represent a serious technological advance over all existing Soviet fighters. The MiG-21 'Fishbed' had been agile by the standards of its day, but its size left it deficient in range, armament, and growth potential. The MiG-23 'Flogger', developed to match the F-4 Phantom II, was fast and had more space for fuel and equipment, but its maneuverability and dog fighting ability were deficient. The Soviets clearly needed a better-balanced fighter with both agility and sophisticated systems. In response, the Soviet General Staff issued a requirement for a Perspektivnyi Frontovoi Istrebitel (PFI, roughly 'advanced tactical fighter'). It was extremely ambitious, calling for long range, good short-field performance (including the ability to use austere runways), excellent agility, Mach 2+ speed, and heavy armament. The aerodynamic design for the new aircraft was largely carried out by TsAGI, the Russian aerodynamics institute, in collaboration with Sukhoi. In 1971 the Soviets determined that the PFI aircraft would be too expensive to procure in the quantities needed (directly paralleling the contemporary USAF experience that led to the Lightweight Fighter program and the F-16 Fighting Falcon and YF-17 Cobra), and divided it into TPFI (Tyazholyi Perspektivnyi Frontovoi Istrebitel, heavy advanced tactical fighter) and LPFI (Legkiy Perspektivnyi Frontovoi Istrebitel, lightweight advanced tactical fighter).

EUROFIGHTER TYPHOON

The Eurofighter Typhoon is a twin-engine multi-role canard-delta strike fighter aircraft, designed and built by a consortium of European aerospace manufacturers, Eurofighter GmbH, formed in 1986. The series production of the Eurofighter Typhoon is underway, and the aircraft is being procured under three separate contracts (referred to as "tranches"), each for aircraft with generally improved capabilities. The aircraft has entered service with the British Royal Air Force, the German Luftwaffe, the Italian Air Force, the Spanish Air Force and the Austrian Air Force. Saudi Arabia has signed a £4.43 billion contract for 72 aircraft.

The Typhoon features foreplanes, and lightweight construction. The fighter achieves high agility at both supersonic and low speeds by having a relaxed stability design. It has a quadruplex digital fly-by-wire control system providing artificial stability, as manual operation alone could not compensate for the inherent instability. The fly-by-wire system is described as "carefree" by preventing the pilot from exceeding the permitted manoeuvre envelope. Although not designated a stealth fighter, measures were taken to reduce the Typhoon's radar cross section (RCS), especially from the frontal aspect. An example of these measures is that the Typhoon has jet inlets that conceal the front of the jet engine (a strong radar target) from radar. Many important potential radar targets, such as the wing, canard and fin leading edges, are highly swept, so will reflect radar energy well away from the front sector. Some external weapons are mounted semi-recessed into the aircraft, partially shielding these missiles from incoming radar waves.

F-4 PHANTOM

The McDonnell Douglas F-4 Phantom II (Model 98) is a two-place (tandem), supersonic, long-range, all-weather fighter-bomber. An unmistakable icon of the Cold War and the first modern air superiority fighter, the Phantom entered service with US military in the early 1960s and remains on active duty in several countries to this day. Shortly after its debut, the aircraft broke 16 world records for speed and altitude. The Phantom expanded its original air defense role to include tactical reconnaissance and ground attack with conventional and nuclear munitions. The Phantom was the only aircraft used by both the USAF Thunderbirds (F-4E) and the US Navy Blue Angels (F-4J) flight demonstration teams.

The McDonnell F-4 Phantom II origins trace back to the 1953 proposal for an upgraded F3H Demon. Although Vought F-8 Crusader won the Navy contract, the Super Demon was developed into a ground attack AH-1, which by 1955 had evolved into an all-weather air superiority F4H. The F4H first flew in 1958 and remained in production from 1959 until 1981. Dave Lewis was the chief of preliminary design, and ultimately, the Program Manager for the development and sales effort. In air combat, Phantom's greatest advantage was its excellent thrust which permitted a skilled pilot to engage and disengage from the fight at will. Not surprisingly, the massive aircraft lacked the agility of its Soviet opponents. Although the F-4 proved somewhat liable to enter spins during high-G and high angle of attack maneuvers, pilots reported the aircraft to be very communicative and easy to fly on the edge of its performance envelope.

MIRAGE 2000

The Mirage 2000 is a French-built multi-role fighter manufactured by Dassault Aviation. The true origin of the Mirage 2000 is the less-known Mirage 4000, a twin engine delta air interceptor that was a private venture from Dassault, and was very capable. The Royal Saudi Air Force was very interested, but eventually it dropped from the project in favor of the American F-15. As a result of this lost sale, Dassault built a scaled down, less expensive, but still very capable version of the 4000: the Mirage 2000. Its first role is to be an interceptor, yet it retains a ground-attack capability. Using only the basic concept of the delta interceptor previously seen on the classic Mirage III, Dassault built a totally new design. Using fly-by-wire controls and relaxed stability, Dassault was capable of bringing the classic delta to a new level, with loads up to 12g's (for short periods of time, the default is 9g's), a more powerful engine (but not so powerful as the latest American engines, an old problem the French aircraft industries were still not able to overcome). Development began on the aircraft in the 1970s and the first flight took place in 1978. By 1983 it began seeing service in the French Air Force. The Mirage 2000 has many variants. The first operational Mirage 2000 was the 2000C, using first the stopgap RDM radar, and later the definitive RDI digital radar. The evolution of the 2000 came with the Mirage 2000-5, with much improved RDY radar, glass cockpit, MICA fire-and-forget BVR missiles and numerous other improvements. The Mirage 2000 has a maximum speed of Mach 2.2. More than 500 have been produced. After the French Air Force, the Indian Air Force (IAF) fields the greatest number of Mirage 2000 aircraft.

TORNADO

The Panavia Tornado is a family of twin-engine combat aircraft, which was jointly developed by the United Kingdom, West Germany and Italy. There are three primary versions of the Tornado; the Tornado IDS (Interdictor/Strike) fighter-bomber, the suppression of enemy air defences Tornado ECR (Electronic Combat/ Reconnaissance) and the Tornado ADV (Air Defence Variant) interceptor. It is one of the world's most sophisticated and capable interdiction and attack aircraft, with a large payload, long range and high survivability.

The Tornado was designed as a low-level supersonic ground attack bomber, capable of taking off and landing in short distances. This requires good high-speed and low-speed flying characteristics. In general, an aircraft which is designed to fly at high speeds usually has poor low-speed characteristics. In order to achieve the desired high-speed performance, an aircraft has a highly swept or 'delta' wing platform. However, these wing designs are very inefficient at low speeds where unswept wing planforms are required. In order for an aircraft to be operated efficiently at both high and low speeds, variable wing sweep is a desirable feature; this was incorporated into the Tornado design. When the wings are swept back, the Tornado IDS increases its high-speed low-level capability by reducing drag. When sweeping, the wings partially slide into the fuselage, reducing the exposed wing area. This gives the aircraft a low gust response in turbulent low-level winds. This not only makes flight much more comfortable for the aircrew but also makes the aircraft a more stable platform from which to aim and deliver unguided weapons at low level.

CONCORDE

The Aérospatiale-BAC Concorde aircraft was a turbojet-powered supersonic passenger airliner, a supersonic transport (SST). It was a product of an Anglo-French government treaty, combining the manufacturing efforts of Aérospatiale and the British Aircraft Corporation. First flown in 1969, Concorde entered service in 1976 and continued for 27 years. Concorde flew regular transatlantic flights from London Heathrow (British Airways) and Paris-Charles de Gaulle Airport (Air France) to New York JFK and Washington Dulles, profitably flying these routes at record speeds, in less than half the time of other airliners. Indeed, Concorde held many speed records. With only 20 aircraft built, the costly development phase represented a substantial economic loss. Additionally, Air France and British Airways were subsidised by their governments to buy the aircraft. As a result of the type's only crash (on 25 July 2000), world economic effects arising from the 9/11 attacks, and other factors, operations ceased on 24 October 2003. The last "retirement" flight occurred on 26 November 2003. Concorde was an ogival (also "ogee") delta-winged aircraft with four Olympus engines based on those originally developed for the Avro Vulcan strategic bomber. The engines were jointly built by Rolls-Royce and SNECMA. Concorde was the first civil airliner to have an analogue fly-by-wire flight control system. It also employed a trademark droop snoot lowering nose section for visibility on approach. These and other features permitted Concorde to have an average cruise speed of Mach 2.02 (about 2,140 km/h or 1,330 mph) with a maximum cruise altitude of 18,300 metres (60,000 feet), more than twice the speed of conventional aircraft. The average landing speed was 298 km/h (185 mph, 160 knots).

F-16 FALCON

The F-16 Fighting Falcon is a modern multi-role jet fighter, developed by General Dynamics in the United States. Initially designed as a lightweight fighter, the plane has evolved into a successful multi-role aircraft. The Falcon's versatility is the primary reason that it is success on the export market, currently serving 24 countries. It is the largest and probably most significant Western fighter program, with over 4000 aircraft built. Though no longer produced for the United States Air Force, it is still produced for export. The F-16 originated in a set of specifications by the United States Department of Defense. The deficiencies of the F-4 Phantom II in aerial combat in the Vietnam War, particularly at close ranges, shaped the specifications for the F-15 Eagle. An informal and influential group nicknamed the "Fighter Mafia", among them systems analyst Pierre Sprey, test pilot Charles E. Meyers, test pilot Everest Riccioni, and former instructor pilot John Boyd, believed the F-15 was a move in the wrong direction. They argued that the F-15 was too large and expensive. Designed as a fast interceptor, it had a wide turn radius and was not well suited to close range dogfighting. The Fighter Mafia argued for a lighter fighter with superb maneuverability, that was cheap enough to deploy in numbers. These specifications became the Lightweight Fighter (LWF) program, begun in 1971. The Fighting Falcon is regarded as a superb dogfighter, with innovations such as the bubble canopy, side-mounted control stick, and reclined seat. It was also the first US fighter aircraft to match the English Electric Lightning's ability to execute 9 g turns. Although the F-16's official popular name is "Fighting Falcon", it is known to its pilots as the "Viper", the General Dynamics codename for the project during its early development.

F-35 JOINT STRIKE FIGHTER

The JSF exists in three primary variants. The F-35A, F-35B, and F-35C. For the JSF Trials, only the F-35A and F-35B models were demonstrated. The F-35A is the smallest, lightest version, which uses conventional takeoff and landing. The F-35A variant is intended for use primarily by the U.S. Air Force. The F-35C is the largest F-35, with the largest wingspan and the heaviest, most reinforced fuselage. The F-35C is intended for use as a carrier based aircraft, the larger wing area allowing more control at low carrier landing velocities and high glide angles, and the reinforced fuselage required for the extremes of carrier arrested landings and catapult launches. The final F-35 variant is the F-35B VSTOL aircraft, often referred to as the F-35 Marine version. The F-35B is clearly intended to replace the U.S. Marine Corps' AV-8B Harrier strike jets, while retaining common parts with other F-35 aircraft. F-35B is capable of vertical take-off and landing.

The F-35 powerplant uses the highly complex Remote Shaft-Driven Lift Fan concept. Turbine power is diverted forward via a clutch-and-bevel gearbox, to a vertically mounted, contra-rotating lift fan located forward of the main engine in the center of the aircraft. Bypass air from the turbofan exhausts through a pair of roll post nozzles on either side of the fuselage, while both the lift fan and the LP turbine streams exhaust through thrust vectoring nozzles. In effect, the F-35 power plant acts as a flow multiplier and consequently has more than sufficient thrust for lift operations. This lift concept has the additional benefit of lowering environmental effects during (primarily) landing, where the thermal effects on, for example, a carrier deck are greatly reduced.

FA-18 HORNET

The F/A-18 Hornet is a modern all-weather carrier strike fighter. Designed in the 1970s, the plane is in service with the U.S. Navy and U.S. Marine Corps, as well as many other armed forces across the globe. It fills the roles of fighter escort, fleet air defense, suppression of enemy air defenses (SEAD), interdiction, close and deep air support, reconnaissance, and forward air control. Its versatility and reliability have proven it to be a valuable carrier asset. Its drawbacks include its relative lack of range and speed, and its inability to land on aircraft carriers with significant combat loads.

The F/A-18 is a twin engine, mid-wing, multi-mission tactical aircraft. It is superbly maneuverable, owing to its good thrust to weight ratio, digital fly-by-wire control system, and leading edge extensions (LEX). The LEX allow the Hornet to remain controllable at high angles of attack. This is because the LEX produce powerful vortices over the wings, creating turbulent airflow and thus delaying or eliminating the aerodynamic separation responsible for stall. The Hornet was among the first aircraft to heavily utilize multi-function displays, which at the switch of a button allow the pilot to perform either fighter or attack roles or both. This "force multiplier" capability gives the operational commander more flexibility in employing tactical aircraft in a rapidly changing battle scenario. It was the first Navy aircraft to incorporate a digital multiplex avionics bus, enabling easy upgrades. The Hornet is also notable for having been designed with maintenance in mind, and as a result has required far less downtime than its counterparts, the F-14 Tomcat and the A-6 Intruder. Its mean time between failure is three times greater than any other Navy strike aircraft, and requires half the maintenance time.

JAGUAR

The SEPECAT Jaguar is an Anglo-French ground attack aircraft in service with the Royal Air Force and several export customers, notably the Indian Air Force. The aircraft served as one French Air Force's main strike aircraft until July 1, 2005 when it was replaced by Dassault Rafale. It was the product of the world's first bi-national military aircraft program.

The Jaguar program began in the early 1960s, in response to a British requirement for an advanced supersonic jet trainer, and a French need for a cheap, subsonic dual role trainer and attack aircraft with good short field performance. From these apparently disparate aims would come a single and entirely different aircraft: relatively high-tech, supersonic, and optimised for ground attack in a high-threat environment. It was planned as a replacement for the RAF Hawker Hunter and the Armee de l'Air F-100 Super Sabre. Cross-channel negotiations led to the formation of SEPECAT (the Société Européenne de Production de l'Avion d'Ecole de Combat et d'Appui Tactique) in 1966 as a joint venture between Bréguet (the design leader) and the British Aircraft Corporation to produce the airframe, and a separate teaming of Rolls-Royce and Turboméca to develop the Adour afterburning turbofan engine. The first of 8 prototypes flew on September 8 1968. It was an orthodox single-seat, swept-wing, twin-engine design but with tall landing gear. It had a maximum take-off weight in the 15 tonne class and could manage a combat radius on internal fuel alone of 850 km. Maximum speed was Mach 1.6 (Mach 1.1 at sea level) and hardpoints were fitted for an external weapons load of up to 10 000 lb.

B-1B LANCER

The Boeing IDS (formerly Rockwell) B-1B Lancer is a long-range strategic bomber in service with the United States Air Force (USAF). Together with the B-52 Stratofortress and the B-2 Spirit, it is the backbone of the United States's long-range bomber force. The B-1 was conceived as the Advanced Manned Strategic Aircraft (AMSA) program circa 1965. After a prolonged development period, the contract was awarded in 1970 to Rockwell International. The first of four prototype B-1A models (s/n 74-158) flew on December 23, 1974. Intended as a high-speed, long-range bomber capable of a supersonic low-level dash and Mach 2.5 at altitude, the B-1A never went into production. The program was cancelled by decision of President Jimmy Carter in 1977, although flight tests of the four B-1A models continued through 1981.

The first B-1A was scrapped at the Rome Air Development Center, New York. The second (s/n 74-159) flew for the subsequent B-1B program, but crashed on August 29, 1984. This aircraft was equipped with a crew escape capsule, instead of conventional ejection seats. The capsule ejected from the aircraft, but the parachute deployed improperly and the pilot, Doug Benefield, was killed on impact. The other two B-1As survive. The third prototype (s/n 74-160) is on display at Wings Over the Rockies in Denver, Colorado. The last B-1A (s/n 74-174) also served in the B-1B program. It was on display at the National Museum of the United States Air Force near Dayton, Ohio for many years before moving to the Strategic Air and Space Museum in Ashland, Nebraska. This aircraft has conventional ejection seats and other features distinctive to the B-1B variant instead of the B-1A.

F-117 NIGHTHAWK

The Lockheed F-117A Nighthawk is the world's first operational aircraft completely designed around stealth technology. Flown only by the United States Air Force, it is a direct descendant of the Have Blue stealth prototype program. The F-117A was widely publicized during the Gulf War. It is scheduled to be replaced by the F-22 Raptor between 2008 and 2020. About the size of an F-15C Eagle, the single-seat, twin-engine F-117A is powered by two non-afterburning General Electric F404 turbofan engines, and has quadruple-redundant fly-by-wire flight controls. It is air refuelable. In order to lower development costs, the avionics, fly-by-wire systems, and other parts are derived from the F-16 Fighting Falcon and F/A-18 Hornet. Among the penalties for stealth are 30% lower engine power and a very low wing aspect ratio, thanks to the high sweep angle needed to deflect incoming radar waves to the sides. The F-117A is equipped with sophisticated navigation and attack systems integrated into a digital avionics suite. It carries no radar, which lowers emissions and cross-section. It navigates primarily by GPS and high-accuracy inertial navigation. Missions are coordinated by an automated planning system that can automatically perform all aspects of a strike mission, including weapons release. Targets are acquired by a thermal imaging infrared system, slaved to a laser that finds the range and designates targets for laser-guided bombs. It can theoretically carry two examples of nearly any weapon in the USAF inventory, including the B61 nuclear bomb. There are a number of bombs that it cannot carry, either because they are too large to fit, or are incompatible with the F-117's carry system.

BOEING 727

The Boeing 727 is a mid-size, narrow-body, three-engine, T-tailed commercial jet airliner. The first Boeing 727 flew in 1963 and for over a decade it was the most produced commercial jet airliner in the world. When production ended in 1984, a total of 1,831 aircraft had been produced. The 727's sales record for the most jet airliners ever sold was broken in the early 1990s by its younger stablemate, the Boeing 737.

The 727 was produced following the success of the Boeing 707 quad-jet airliner. Designed for short-haul routes, the 727 became a mainstay of airlines' domestic route networks. A stretched variant, the 727-200, debuted in 1967. In August 2008, there were a total of 81 Boeing 727-100 aircraft and 419 727-200 aircraft in airline service. The 727 is one of the noisiest commercial jetliners, categorized as Stage 2 by the U.S. Noise Control Act of 1972, which mandated the gradual introduction of quieter Stage 3 aircraft. The 727's JT8D jet engines use older low-bypass turbofan technology while Stage 3 aircraft utilize the more efficient and quieter high-bypass turbofan design. When the Stage 3 requirement was being proposed, Boeing engineers analyzed the possibility of incorporating quieter engines on the 727. They determined that the JT8D-200 engine could be used on the two side-mounted pylons, but the structural work required to fit the larger-diameter engine into the fuselage structure at the number two engine location would be too great to be justifiable. At the turn of the 21st century, the 727 was still in service with a few airline fleets. However, due to changes by the U.S. FAA and the ICAO in over-water flight requirements, most major airlines had already begun to switch to twin-engine aircraft, which are more fuel-efficient and quieter than the three-engine 727.

DASSAULT FALCON 900

The Dassault Falcon 900 is a French-built corporate jet aircraft made by Dassault Aviation. It, along with its larger sibling the Falcon 7X, are the only trijets currently in production. Both aircraft are notable in featuring an S-duct central engine. . The Falcon 900 is a development of the Falcon 50, itself a development of the earlier Falcon 20. The Falcon 900 development included computer-aided design and the incorporation of composite materials. Improved models include the Falcon 900B, featuring improved engines and increased range, and the Falcon 900EX featuring further improvements in engines and range and an all-glass flight deck. The Falcon 900C is a lower-cost companion to the Falcon 900EX and replaces the Falcon 900B. The current versions are the Falcon 900EX EASy and the Falcon 900DX. At EBACE 2008, the Falcon 900LX incorporates High Mach Blended Winglets designed by Aviation Partners Inc. The same winglets are being developed for the entire Falcon 900 series as a retrofit kit with certification planned for 2009. The 900LX flies 4,800 nautical miles nonstop, the farthest in its class. And with its classic trijet engine design, the 900LX can use small airports at high altitudes, even on hot days. It's the most versatile aircraft and also one of the safest given its ability to fly slower on approach than its twinjet competitors. The Falcon can climb directly to 39,000 feet putting you above most weather and traffic and fly directly to far off places unrestricted by ETOPS (Extended Twin-Engine Operations) considerations. The Falcon 900LX can link Mumbai to London, Paris to Beijing, New York to Moscow, Los Angeles to Dublin, landing with NBAA IFR reserves

B-52 STRATOFORTRESS

The Boeing B-52 Stratofortress is a long-range eight-engined strategic bomber flown by the United States Air Force (USAF) since 1954, replacing the Convair B-36 and the Boeing B-47. Although built for the role of Cold War-era nuclear deterrent, its conventional capabilities are these days the more important role in USAF operations, where its long range, heavy weapons load and comparatively economical operation (compared to the rest of the USAF strategic bomber fleet) are extremely useful. For more than 50 years, the B-52 Stratofortress has been the backbone of the manned strategic bomber force for the United States. The B-52 is capable of dropping or launching a wide array of weapons in the U.S. inventory, including free-fall (gravity bombs), cluster bombs, and precision guided ordnance such as Joint Direct Attack Munitions. When updated with the latest technology, the B-52 will be capable of delivering the full complement of joint developed weapons; allowing it to continue well into the 21st century as an important element of U.S. military capabilities. Current engineering analyses show the B-52's life span to extend beyond the year 2045. The B-52A first flew in August 1954 and the B model entered service in 1955. A total of 744 B-52s were built with the last, a B-52H, delivered in October 1962. Only the H model is still in the Air Force inventory and is assigned to Air Combat Command and the Air Force Reserves. The oldest B-52 still flying was a B-52B that was built in 1955, though it also has the fewest flight hours of any surviving B-52. It was operated by NASA's Dryden Flight Research Center and was used for drop tests of various research aircraft until its retirement on December 17, 2004. On July 30, 2001, Dryden received a B-52H that is expected to fully replace the older B-model aircraft by the end of 2004.

AIRBUS A380

The Airbus A380 is a double-deck, wide-body, four-engine airliner manufactured by the European corporation Airbus, an EADS subsidiary. The largest passenger airliner in the world, the A380 made its maiden flight on 27 April 2005 from Toulouse, France, and made its first commercial flight on 25 October 2007 from Singapore to Sydney with Singapore Airlines. The A380 is offered in passenger and freighter versions. The A380-800, the passenger model, is the largest passenger airliner in the world, superseding the Boeing 747, but has a shorter fuselage than the Airbus A340-600 which is Airbus' next biggest passenger aeroplane. The A380-800 has a design range of 15,200 kilometres (8,200 nmi), sufficient to fly from New York to Hong Kong for example, and a cruising speed of Mach 0.85 (about 900 km/h or 560 mph at cruise altitude). The development cost of the A380 had grown to €11 billion when the first aircraft was completed.

Boeing, meanwhile, resurrected the 747X programme several times before finally launching the 747-8 Intercontinental in November 2005 (with entry into service planned for 2009). Boeing chose to develop a derivative for the 400 to 500 seat market, instead of matching the A380's capacity.

Major structural sections of the A380 are built in France, Germany, Spain, and the United Kingdom. Due to their size, they are brought to the assembly hall in Toulouse in France by surface transportation, rather than by the A300-600ST Beluga aircraft used for other Airbus models. Components of the A380 are provided by suppliers worldwide; the five largest contributors, by value, are Rolls-Royce, SAFRAN, United Technologies, General Electric, and Goodrich.

AIRBUS A320

The Airbus A320 family of short- to medium-range commercial passenger airliners are manufactured by Airbus. Family members include the A318, A319, A320, and A321, as well as the ACJ business jet. First delivered in 1988, the A320 pioneered the use of digital fly-by-wire flight control systems in a commercial aircraft. With more than 3,000 aircraft of the A320 family built, it is the second best-selling jet airliner family of all time after the family's primary competition, the Boeing 737. The A320 was targeted at the global fleet replacement requirements for the 727 and early variants of the 737. After the oil price rises of the 1970s, Airbus needed to minimise the trip fuel costs of the A320. To that end, Airbus incorporated advanced features including fly-by-wire flight control, composite primary structures, centre-of-gravity control using fuel, glass cockpit (EFIS) and a two-person flight deck. The end result was that the A320 consumes 50% less fuel than the 727. The Airbus A320s sold to China to be delivered between 2009 and 2012 will be assembled in the People's Republic of China in Tianjin. The A320 family has the highest production rate ever for any commercial airliner. In response to continuing strong demand, Airbus continues its steady production ramp-up programme from 30 aircraft per month reached at the end of 2006, to 32 in early 2007, 34 in March 2008, 36 in December 2008, 38 in mid 2009 and 40 by the end of 2009. The A320 features a computerised on-board maintenance system. The flight deck is equipped with EFIS with sidestick controllers. Two suppliers provide turbofan engines for the A320 series: CFM International with their CFM56, and International Aero Engines, offering the V2500.

BOEING 707

The Boeing 707 is a four-engine commercial passenger jet airliner developed by Boeing in the early 1950s. Its name is most commonly pronounced as "Seven Oh Seven". Boeing delivered a total of 1,010 Boeing 707s, which dominated passenger air transport in the 1960s and remained common through the 1970s. The first flight of the first production 707-120 took place on December 20, 1957, and FAA certification followed on September 18, 1958.[6] A number of changes were incorporated into the production models from the prototype. A Krueger flap was installed along the leading edge. The height of the vertical fin was increased, and a small fin was added to the underside of the fuselage, and acted as a bumper during excessively nose high takeoffs. While the initial standard model was the 707-120 with JT3C engines, Qantas ordered a shorter body version called the 707-138 and Braniff ordered the higher-thrust version with Pratt & Whitney JT4A engines, the 707-220. The final major derivative was the 707-320 which featured an extended-span wing and JT4A engines, while the 707-420 was the same as the -320 but with Rolls-Royce Conway turbofan engines. British certification requirements relating to engine-out go-arounds also forced Boeing to increase the height of the tail fin on all 707 variants, as well as add a ventral fin. Pan Am was the first airline to operate the 707; the aircraft's first commercial flight was from New York to Paris on October 26, 1958 with a fuel stop in Gander, Newfoundland. American Airlines operated the first domestic 707 flight on January 25, 1959. Continental Airlines introduced its first two 707 aircraft into scheduled service three months later--the first U.S. carrier to employ the type widely in domestic service.

B-2 SPIRIT

The B-2 Spirit, made by Northrop Grumman, is an American multi-role stealth bomber able to drop conventional and nuclear weapons. The B-2 is the most expensive plane ever built. Estimates for the costs per plane range from $1.157 billion USD to $2.2 billion. Its stealth technology is intended to help it penetrate defenses previously impenetrable by combat aircraft. The original procurement of 135 aircraft was later reduced to 75 in the late 1980s. Finally, President George H. W. Bush reduced the final buy quantity to the 21 already bought in his now famous "New World Order" State of the Union speech, January 1991. An estimated 23 billion dollars was secretly spent for research and development on the B-2 in the 1980s. Because the development of the B-2 was one of the best kept secrets of all USAF programs, there was no opportunity for public criticism of its massive cost during development. The first B-2 was publicly displayed on November 22, 1988, when it was rolled out of its hangar at Air Force Plant 42, Palmdale, California, where it was built. Its first flight was on July 17, 1989. The B-2 Combined Test Force, Air Force Flight Test Center, Edwards Air Force Base, California, is responsible for flight testing the engineering, manufacturing and development aircraft. Questions remain over the rising cost of the program . The expense may also be partially explained by the small number of planes produced coupled with a large research overhead in the B-2 program.These bombers were originally designed to drop nuclear weapons during the Cold War and support for them dwindled as military spending declined. In May of 1995, in a study commissioned by Congress, the Institute For Defense Analysis concluded that after the demise of the Soviet Union, there was no need for more B-2s.

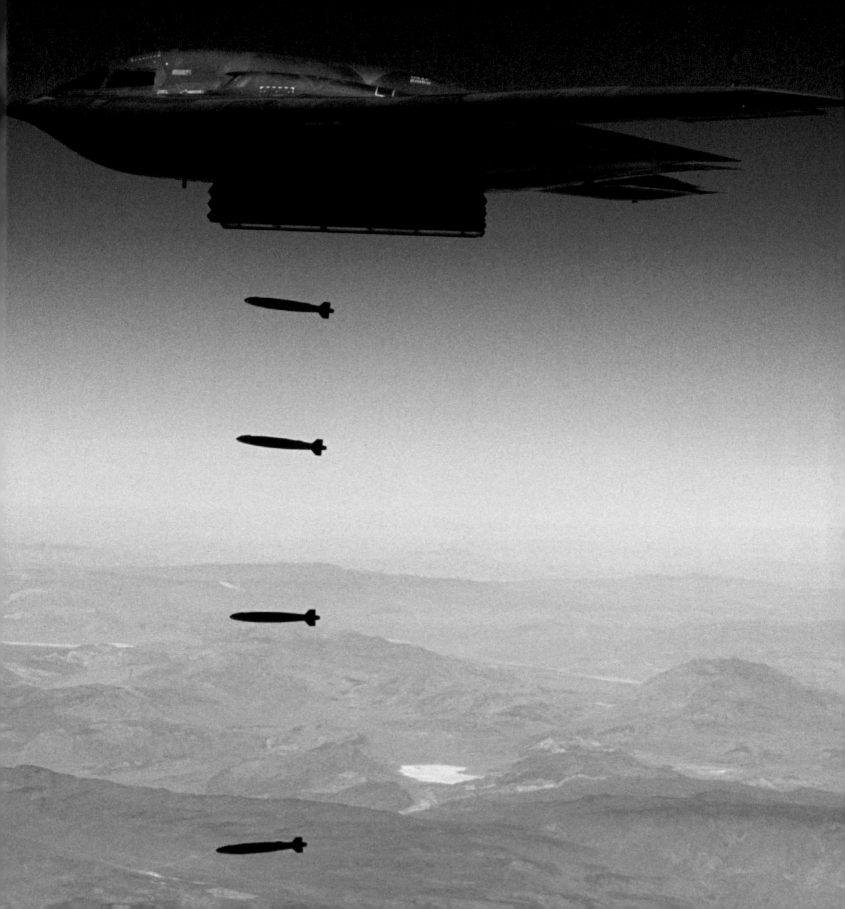

BOEING 747

The Boeing 747, aka the "Jumbo Jet", is among the world's most recognizable aircraft, and was the first wide-body commercial airliner ever produced. First flown commercially in 1970, it held the passenger capacity record for 37 years, until it was surpassed by the Airbus A380. The four-engine 747 uses a double deck configuration for part of its length. It is available in passenger, freighter and other versions. Boeing designed the 747's hump-like upper deck to serve as a first class lounge or (as is the general rule today) extra seating, and to allow the aircraft to be easily converted to a cargo carrier by removing seats and installing a front cargo door. As of June 2009, 1,416 aircraft have been built, with 107 more in various configurations remaining on order. The 747-400, the latest version in service, is among the fastest airliners in service with a high-subsonic cruise speed of Mach 0.85 (567 mph or 913 km/h). It has an intercontinental range of 7,260 nautical miles (8,350 mi or 13,450 km). The 747-400 passenger version can accommodate 416 passengers in a typical three-class layout or 524 passengers in a typical two-class layout. The next version of the aircraft, the 747-8, is in production and scheduled to enter service in 2010. The 747 is to be replaced by the Boeing Y3 (part of the Boeing Yellowstone Project) in the future.

GULFSTREAM G650

The Gulfstream G650 is an ultra-large-cabin, ultra-high speed business jet. The flagship of the Gulfstream fleet flies faster and farther than any traditional business aircraft and envelops its privileged passengers in a level of comfort far greater than any other aircraft in its class.

Introduced in 2008, the G650 will carry eight passengers and a crew of four on nonstop legs of 7,000 nautical miles. That means it will link Dubai with New York and London with Buenos Aires. With its powerful Rolls-Royce BR725 engines, the G650 will cover shorter distances at a speed of Mach 0.925. No traditional business jet will take you closer to the speed of sound. Exceptional power and ultra-long legs aside, the G650 will be remarkably versatile. It will deliver excellent takeoff and landing performance with a balanced field length of just 6,000 feet. The G650 is the most technologically advanced business aircraft in the sky. The G650 comes standard with many advanced safety features such as Enhanced Vision System II™, the Head-Up Display II and the Synthetic Vision-Primary Flight Display. Its Planeview II™ cockpit comes equipped with a Triplex Flight Management System, Automatic Emergency Descent Mode, 3-D weather radar, Advanced Flight Controls – in short, a full array of sophisticated, next-generation technology to improve pilot situational awareness and enhance safety.

BOMBARDIER GLOBAL EXPRESS

Bombardier Aerospace began studies in 1991 and the aircraft was officially launched in 1993. The first flight occurred on October 13, 1996.

The Global Express can fly intercontinental ranges without refueling (e.g. New York - Tokyo) or between most two points in the world with only one stop. In this class the Global Express competes with the Airbus Corporate Jet, Boeing Business Jet, Dassault Falcon 7X and Gulfstream G550. Bombardier subsidiaries have three specific roles in the project: Canadair is the design leader and manufactures the nose; Short Brothers, Belfast is responsible for the design and manufacture of the engine nacelles, horizontal stabiliser and forward fuselage; and de Havilland Canada builds the rear fuselage and vertical tail and carries out final assembly. The major external supplier is Japan's Mitsubishi Heavy Industries which builds the wing and centre fuselage sections.

The Global Express is powered by two Rolls-Royce BR710 turbofans. The Global Express XRS is an improved version of the original aircraft, offering higher cruise speed, increased range, improved cabin layout and lighting. It is reported that the letters have no significance, but were chosen by focus groups simply to improve the brand image. The range increase is achieved by addition of a 1,486 lb (674 kg) fuel tank at the wing root. The Global Express XRS entered service in early 2006. The unit price is estimated to be $45.5 million (US). Bombardier claims it takes 15 minutes less to fuel the XRS than the original model thanks to improved computer systems and mechanical refinements.

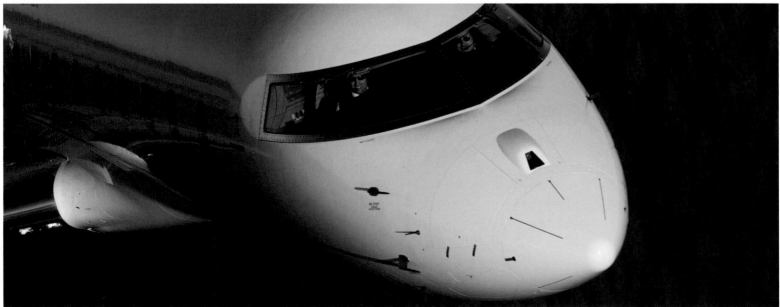

BOEING 777

The Boeing 777 is an American long-range, wide-body twin-engine airliner built by Boeing Commercial Airplanes. The world's largest twinjet and commonly referred to as the "Triple Seven", it can carry between 283 and 368 passengers in a three-class configuration and has a range from 5,235 to 9,450 nautical miles (9,695 to 17,500 km). Distinguishing features of the 777 include the six wheels on each main landing gear, its circular fuselage cross section, the largest diameter turbofan engines of any aircraft, the pronounced "neck" aft of the cockpit, and the blade-like tail cone. Singapore Airlines is the largest operator of the Boeing 777 family with 73 in service (46 are the 777-200ER variant, 12 are 777-300s, and 11 are 777-300ERs with 8 on firm order and 13 more on option). As of February 2008, 53 customers have placed orders for 1,050 777s. Direct market competitors to the 777 are the Airbus A330-300, A340, and some variants of the A350 XWB, which is currently under development. The 777 may eventually be replaced by a new product family, the Boeing Y3, which would draw upon technologies from the 787. The Y3 may also replace the Boeing 747 series. In the 1970s, Boeing unveiled new models: the twin-engine 757 to replace the venerable 727, the twin-engine 767 to challenge the Airbus A300, and a trijet 777 concept to compete with the DC-10 and the Lockheed L-1011 TriStar. Based on a re-winged 767 design, the 275 seat 777 was to be offered in two variants: a 2,700 nautical miles (5,000 km) transcontinental and an 4,320 nmi (8,000 km) intercontinental. The twinjets were a big success, due in part to the 1980s ETOPS regulations. The 777 was the first commercial aircraft to be designed entirely on computer. Everything was created on a 3D CAD software system known as CATIA, sourced from Dassault Systemes.

BOEING 787

The Boeing 787 Dreamliner is a mid-sized, wide-body, twin engine jet airliner currently under development by Boeing Commercial Airplanes. It carries between 210 and 330 passengers depending on variant and seating configuration. Boeing stated that it will be more fuel-efficient than earlier Boeing airliners and will be the first major airliner to use composite materials for most of its construction. Boeing's development of the 787 is also innovative in the collaborative management approach with suppliers. On January 28, 2005, the aircraft's development designation 7E7 was changed to the 787. Early released concept images depicted a radical design with highly curved surfaces. On April 26, 2005, a year after the launch of the program, the final look of the external 787 design was frozen, with a less rakish nose and a more conventional tail. Boeing featured its first 787 in a rollout ceremony on July 8, 2007 at its assembly factory in Everett, Washington, by which time it had become the fastest-selling wide body airliner in history with nearly 600 orders. Originally scheduled to enter service in May 2008, production has been delayed and it is currently scheduled to enter into service in late 2009. In the late 1990s, Boeing began considering a replacement for the 767 when sales weakened due to the competing Airbus A330-200. As sales of the Boeing 747-400 were also slowing, the company proposed two new aircraft, which were the Sonic Cruiser and the 747X. The Sonic Cruiser would have achieved higher speeds (approximately Mach 0.98) while burning fuel at the same rate as the existing 767 or A330. The 747X, competing with the Airbus A380, would have lengthened the 747-400 and improved efficiency by using a composite supercritical wing.

AIRBUS A350

The Airbus A350 is a long range, mid-sized, wide-body family of airliners currently under development, designed to compete with the Boeing 777 and Boeing 787. The A350 will be the first Airbus with fuselage and wing structures made primarily of carbon fiber reinforced plastic. It is scheduled to enter into service in 2013. On 6 October 2005 full industrial launch of the program was announced with an estimated development cost of around $4.5 billion. This version of the A350 was planned to be a 250–300-seat twin-engined wide-body aircraft derived from the design of the existing A330. Under this plan, the A350 would have modified wings and new engines while sharing the same fuselage cross-section as its predecessor. Controversially, the fuselage was to consist primarily of Al-Li, rather than the CFRP fuselage on the 787. It was to see entry into service in 2010 in two versions; the A350-800 capable of flying 8,800 nautical miles (16,300 km) with typical passenger capacity of 253 in 3-class configuration and the 300-seat (3-class) A350-900 with 7,500 nautical mile (13,890 km) range. On September 2007, Airbus rolled out new design advances to a gathering of 100 representatives from existing and potential XWB customers. The A350 XWB will be built on the technologies developed for Airbus A380 and will have a similar cockpit and fly-by-wire systems layout. Airbus claim that 52% of the aircraft will be made out of composites, 20% Al/Al-Li, 14% titanium, 7% steel and 7% the balance. This compares to the Boeing 787, which consists of 50% composites, 20% aluminium, 15% titanium, 10% steel and 5% the balance. October 2008 is the Airbus internal goal to freeze the design and Airbus expects 10% lower airframe maintenance cost and 14% lower empty seat weight than competing aircraft.

BOEING 717

On May 23, 2006, Boeing delivered its final two 717 airplanes to Midwest Airlines and AirTran Airways in a ceremony before thousands of employees, retirees and dignitaries in Long Beach, Calif. The deliveries conclude commercial airplane production in Southern California that began in the 1920s with the Douglas Aircraft Co. The 717 program, which produced 156 airplanes, pioneered breakthrough business and manufacturing processes for Boeing Commercial Airplanes. The program was launched by an order from AirTran Airways in 1995, and the airplane quickly became renowned by customers for its excellent economics, performance and reliability. Based on the Douglas DC-9 and launched as the McDonnell Douglas MD-95, the 100-seater was renamed the Boeing 717 after McDonnell Douglas and Boeing merged in 1997. The 717 will continue to deliver unsurpassed economy and value to our airline customers for years to come. Boeing will continue to provide the outstanding customer service support for the 717s operating at carriers worldwide. Douglas opened the Long Beach factory in 1941 as part of President Roosevelt's Arsenal of Democracy -- a request to the nation's industries to halt civilian production and assist in making wartime equipment. The facility produced almost 10,000 airplanes for World War II before transitioning to commercial airplane production after the war. Douglas merged with the McDonnell Aircraft Company in 1967, forming the McDonnell Douglas Corporation. More than 15,000 airplanes have been produced in the Long Beach factory.

BOEING 767

The Boeing 767 is a mid-size, wide-body twinjet airliner produced by Boeing Commercial Airplanes. Passenger versions of the 767 can carry between 181 and 375 passengers, and have a range of 5,200 to 6,590 nautical miles (9,400 to 12,200 km) depending on variant and seating configuration. The Boeing 767 has been produced in three fuselage lengths. The original 767-200 first entered into airline service in 1982, followed by the 767-300 in 1986, and the 767-400ER in 2000. Extended range versions of the original -200 and -300 models, the 767-200ER and 767-300ER, have been produced with added payload and operating distance capability. The 767-300F, a freighter version, entered service in 1995. The first wide-body twinjet produced by Boeing, the 767 was conceived and designed in tandem with the narrow-body Boeing 757 twinjet. Both airliners share design features and flight decks, enabling pilots to obtain a common type rating to operate the two aircraft. The 767 was the first Boeing wide-body airliner to enter service with a two-person crew flight deck, eliminating the need for a flight engineer. Following in-service indications of its twinjet design reliability, the 767 received regulatory approval allowing extended transoceanic operations beginning in 1985. Through the 1990s, the Boeing 767 became commonly used on medium long-haul routes, and the aircraft has ranked as the most commonly-used airliner for transatlantic flights between the United States and Europe. There have been over 1,000 767s ordered with over 900 delivered as of 2009. The -300/-300ER models are the most popular variants, accounting for approximately two-thirds of all 767s ordered. There were 862 767s in service with 48 different airlines as of December 2008.

AIRBUS A330

The Airbus A330 is a large-capacity, wide-body, medium-to-long-range commercial passenger airliner. It was developed at the same time as the four-engined Airbus A340. The A330's fuselage and wings are virtually identical to those of the smaller A340 variants, although it has different engines. The A330 basic fuselage design is inherited from the Airbus A300, as is the nose/cockpit section and the fly-by-wire system and flightdeck from the A320. Both the A330 and A340 are assembled on the same final assembly line at Toulouse-Blagnac, France. By the end of March 2008, a total of 921 A330s had been ordered and 533 delivered. There are two main variants of the A330. The A330-300 was launched in 1987 with introduction into service in 1993. The A330-200 was launched in 1995, introduced in 1998 and comes in passenger, freighter and tanker versions. The A330-200 was developed to compete with the Boeing 767-300ER. The A330-200 is similar to the A340-200 or a shortened version of the A330-300. With poor sales of the A340-200 (of which only 28 were built), Airbus decided to use the fuselage of the A340-200 with the wings and engines of the A330-300. This significantly improved the economics of the plane and made the model more popular than the four-engined variant. Its vertical fin is taller than that of the A330-300 to restore its effectiveness due to the shorter moment arm of the shorter fuselage. It has additional fuel capacity and, like the A330-300, has a Maximum Take-Off Weight (MTOW) of 233 tonnes. Typical range with 253 passengers in a three-class configuration is 12,500 km (6,750 nautical miles). Power is provided by two General Electric CF6-80E, Pratt & Whitney PW4000 or Rolls-Royce Trent 700 engines. All engines are ETOPS-180 min rated. First customer deliveries, to ILFC/Canada 3000, were in April 1998.

INDEX